YORKSHIRE PEOPLE

CHARLOTTE GRAHAM

AMBERLEY

First published 2022

Amberley Publishing
The Hill, Stroud
Gloucestershire, GL5 4EP

www.amberley-books.com

Copyright © Charlotte Graham, 2022

The right of Charlotte Graham to be identified as the Author of this work has been
asserted in accordance with the Copyrights, Designs and Patents Act 1988.

ISBN 978 1 3981 0514 0 (print)
ISBN 978 1 3981 0515 7 (ebook)

British Library Cataloguing in Publication Data.
A catalogue record for this book is available from the British Library.

Typesetting by SJmagic DESIGN SERVICES, India.
Printed in the UK.

FOREWORDS

I've known Charlotte for some years now and having been really taken by her photography on a *Countryfile* publicity shoot some years ago, I asked her if she would take the photos for a series we filmed for Channel 4 called *Our Farm in the Dales*.

I'm sure you will enjoy being transported into the many different worlds Charlotte has so brilliantly captured in the pages of this book. As a dyslexic myself I've always been drawn to the world of pictures and Charlotte has that great skill of capturing and telling stories through the viewfinder.

Enjoy the visual feast that follows.

Matt Baker MBE

Charlotte has collated a fabulous collection of photographs which really capture the huge diversity of the people of Yorkshire. Beauty, creativity and individuality all shine through and once again confirm that Yorkshire is a fantastic place to be.

Stephen Cottrell, Archbishop of York

INTRODUCTION

2022 has been quite a year for many reasons – of both national and personal significance. It has felt like the first year that we have returned to some kind of normality after the disruption of Covid-19, and as a photographer it has been wonderful to get back out and about to see people returning to the lives, the jobs and the hobbies that they love so much.

And then we have faced history being made as we said goodbye to our Queen and hello to our King, an ending and beginning tied together in ceremony and pageantry. When I photograph people, I try to capture the spirit of the subject; a little of the spark that makes the person who they are.

Hopefully, that is what you will see in this collection of images, with a very distinct kind of spark. A very Yorkshire spark.

I have had the privilege of meeting so many people who keep ancient traditions alive, and help create new traditions. People who are ambassadors for Yorkshire, travelling the world to spread its message, and people who simply have a story to tell of life in 'God's own country'.

I sincerely hope that you enjoy looking at these pictures as much as I have enjoyed taking them.

Charlotte Graham, 2022

ACKNOWLEDGEMENTS

Being a freelance photographer, I travel throughout Yorkshire and work all over the country and in Europe with some amazing and very talented people. The images you see in this book would not have been possible without the help of various people who give me access to sites. The images portray a cross section of people.

A very big thank you to the following people or publications: Matt Fearn, Jason Green, Ben Jones and so many others at *The Daily Telegraph*; the picture editor and staff at *The Times*; the picture editor and staff at *The Guardian*; Nick Howard, Abbi Olive, and the maintenance and gardening staff at Castle Howard; the Yorkshire Air Museum; Jorvik; Sharon Atkinson and Leanne Woodhurst at York Minster; York Museums Trust; Make It York; Newby Hall; Fountains Abbey; Harewood House; Kirklees Light Railway; the team at North York Moors Railway, Luke Hudman and Peter Fisher; RHS Harlow Carr; Jay Commins at Pyper York; the Office of the Archbishop and Elizabeth Addy; Amanda Brown at A2BPR; English Heritage; the National Trust; the Great Yorkshire Show; Harrogate Flower Show and Sam Pilling at Sony UK; Grier at Sony Carlisle, National Union of Journalists; BPPA; the actors, actresses and re-enactors who take so much pride in recreating costumes and heritage dress; Paul Barrett, Katie Canning, Mark Jackson, Andy Deane and the conservators at the Royal Armouries; Titch, my little girl; the publishing staff at Amberley; and all the friends and family that have helped me make this happen, including the ones who are too modest to want a mention.

Whitby Goth Festival

The last deep coal miner – Mr Ward

Royal Armouries staff in Poland

Mary Berry and John Sentamu

Danielle and George Clifford

Andrea Jenkins MP

James and Angela, owners of Toulson Court, voted the 'world's best B&B'

Pro Cast Foundry

Laura Hartley – dressed to impress

The Great Beard Competition, Scarborough

Anthony Springall

Mick Baxter

Scarborough Town Crier Alan Booth MBE

Matthew Pugh – Berties of Bay

Falconer at work

Marsden Silver Prize Band

Scarborough Stories

Brassed off in Halifax

Brexit celebrations, Dewsbury

Just jousting around –
Royal Armouries Leeds

Master stonemason Richard Bossons works
on a plaster maquette of the Queen

Morris dancer, Dewsbury

The North Yorkshire Moors Railway

Newby Hall and the Autumn Flower Show

Vicky and Nick Howard

Countryfile comes to Yorkshire

Competitive sheep shearing

Prayers at the summit, Rylstone Cross

Annabelle Bradley, the Malham Smithy

Optical illusion

Out for a ride at Eden Camp

Carnival, Holmfirth

Come on Andy, catch up!

NHS clap for carers

Auld Lang Syne fell race, Haworth

Well I am watching you – watching me!

The Bald Hiker, Castle Howard

The Artist in the Dales

The Theakston Old Peculier
Crime Writing Festival team

GOLD

Goldsborough Hall

It's just a bit of snow

Taking the alpacas for a walk,
Harewood House

Just relaxing at Harewood House

Christine Talbot

Winter glow at Harlow Carr

The Burning Fool

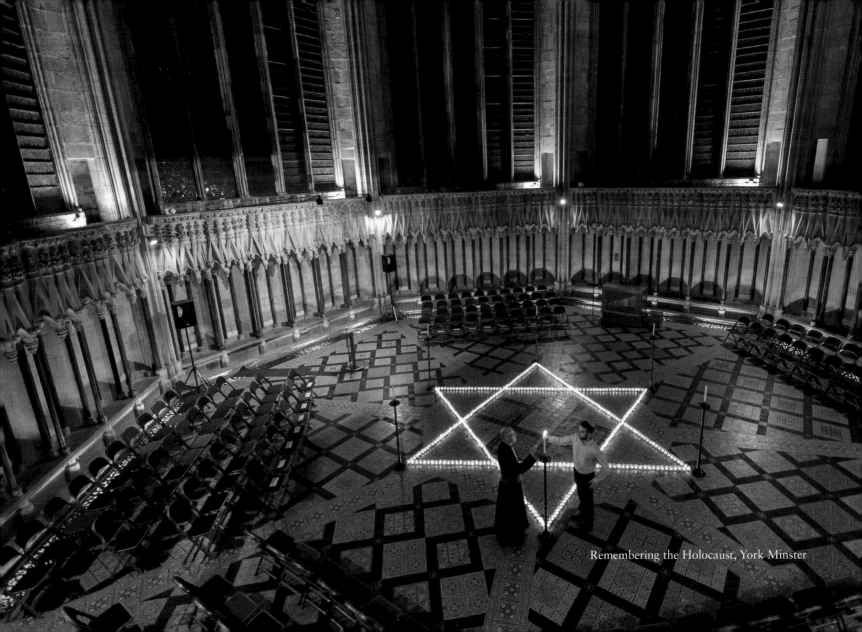

Remembering the Holocaust, York Minster

The Marsden Festival

Imbolc, Marsden

Painting a picture by the river

Jo Moseley, paddleboarder

The Prince and Princess
of Wales visit Bradford

Alan shoots a melon

Flooding in Yorkshire –
well, trying to stop it!

Lobster bathing at the NRM

Farming at Malham

May Day dancing at sunrise

Young apprentice stonemason, York Minster

Maggie lights a candle

Bryony and her daughter
Freya in York

The Archbishop of York, Stephen Cottrell

Clearing the furnace

Liz Truss in Yorkshire

Fixing the boiler on *Sir Nigel Gresley*
at the National Railway Museum, York

Out for a walk

Piglet, North Yorkshire Moors Railway

The team at the North Yorkshire Moors Railway

A young apprentice welding a boiler at
the North Yorkshire Moors Railway

Hebden Bridge Parade

The traditional drag hunt

The Glass-blower

Wensleydale Railway

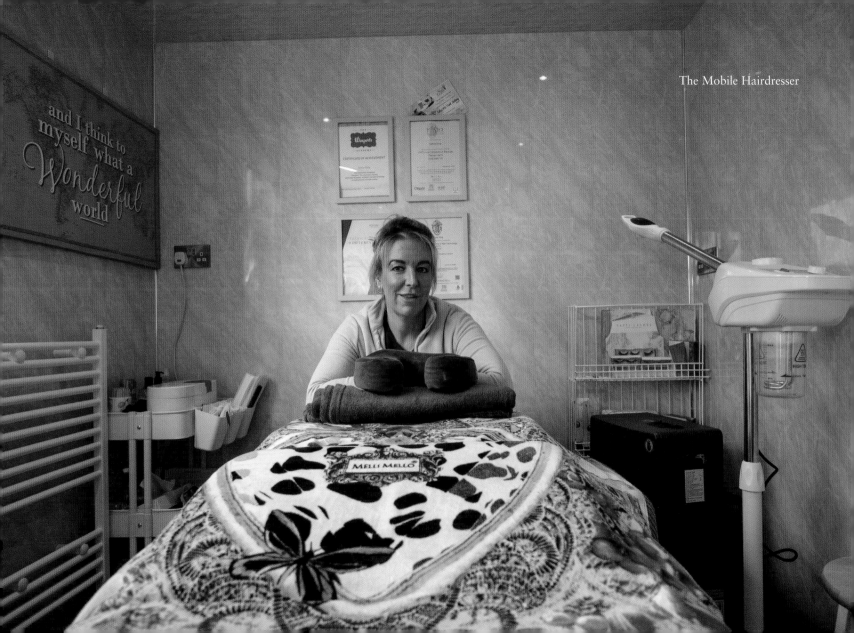

Chris Kamara visits Leeds

Former England captain Gillian Coultard

The Yorkshire Star
Wars Regiment

Give us a hug

All for sale – railway auction

The Kipper Man at Fortune's, Whitby

Harrogate Festivals
Carnival

Ponies on the beach

New Year's Day

The team at the Royal Armouries

Authors, Theakston Old Peculier
Crime Writing Festival

Robert and Paula Tomlinson,
rhubarb growers

No more!

Christmas at the Minster

Corgis for tea

Nick Howard and
Richard Thomson

Look, it's a crane!

Sophie Whittam, fight wear designer

Christmas at Castle Howard –
Percy and Anna

Flooding in York

Superman arrives in York

Latin dancers, Bradford

Tour de Yorkshire

The Easter Bunny

Celebrating VE Day

The Millers of York

Vikings in York

The Steps, Whitby – Goth Festival

The West Yorkshire Police Band

Christmas at the museum, York

York Gate Gardens staff

Ice Cat – ice trail, York

Candle for heroes, Stonefall
Cemetery, Harrogate

Raising the Cross, York Minster

Gary catches the sun